The Big Book Of
PAINTING AND STICKING

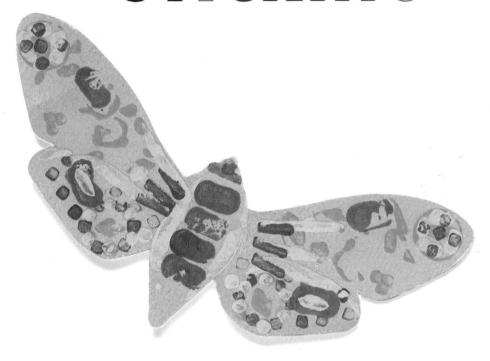

The Big Book Of
PAINTING
AND
STICKING

Jann & Miriam Haworth

MEREHURST

Paint 6

Jann Haworth

CONTENTS

Printing & Stencilling 36
Miriam Haworth

Collage 64
Jann Haworth

Paint

Before you begin the projects in this section, it is a good idea to collect together some useful tools first. You will need scissors for cutting; a pencil, eraser and ruler for drawing and marking out; and glue for fixing things together. You will need paper to paint onto, and, of course, paint. Turn the page for advice on paint-brushes, as well as some other ideas for putting paint on paper.

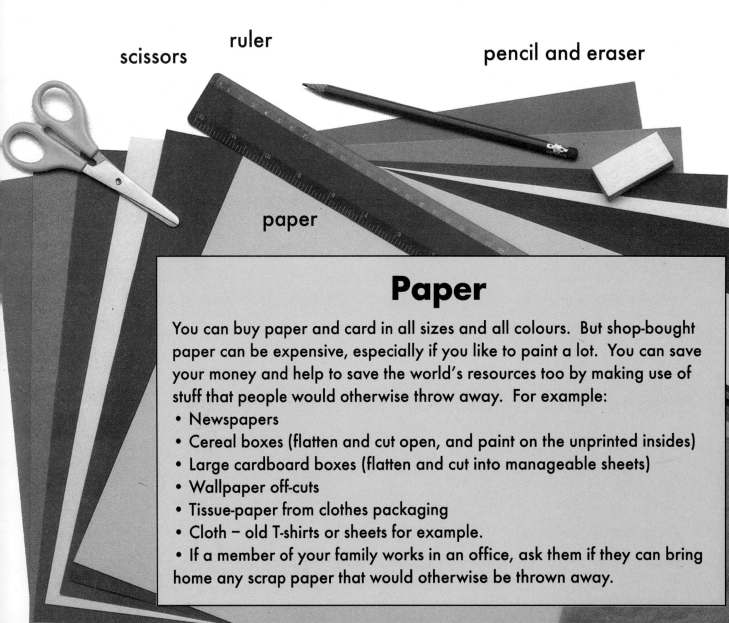

scissors

ruler

pencil and eraser

paper

Paper

You can buy paper and card in all sizes and all colours. But shop-bought paper can be expensive, especially if you like to paint a lot. You can save your money and help to save the world's resources too by making use of stuff that people would otherwise throw away. For example:
• Newspapers
• Cereal boxes (flatten and cut open, and paint on the unprinted insides)
• Large cardboard boxes (flatten and cut into manageable sheets)
• Wallpaper off-cuts
• Tissue-paper from clothes packaging
• Cloth – old T-shirts or sheets for example.
• If a member of your family works in an office, ask them if they can bring home any scrap paper that would otherwise be thrown away.

Paints

Water-based paints have been used for all the projects in this section. You can buy them ready-mixed in large, easy-to-use, squeezy bottles. The basic colours you will need are red, yellow, blue, black and white. From these you can mix all other colours, as you will see on page 10. You can use acrylic paints which come in tubes, but do avoid powder paints: they are dusty, difficult to make up and the colours do not mix well.

Add water to paint to make it thinner or PVA glue to make it thicker.

metal ruler

card

string

masking tape

PVA glue

craft knife

felt-tip pens

water-based paint

acrylic paint

wax crayons

oil-based crayons

tissue-paper

Remember

☆ Wear an apron and cover the work area.
☆ Always ask an adult for help when you see this sign !
☆ Clear up after yourself.

Brush Up On Painting

When you begin to paint, you will need to paint with something. The first thing you might think of is a paint-brush, but there are lots of other things you could use. Blow puddles of thin paint around with a straw. Use your fingers, hands or cut vegetables to print with. Make a card comb and twist it through thick paint, or dabble and smear paint on with a rag. Draw with a twig dipped in thin paint. Last but not least, look at all the different kinds of brushes you could use and try them out for yourself.

plastic straws

plastic comb

twig

card comb

cut potato

roller

hands

newspaper

Useful Things to Collect

All sorts of things around the home can be used to print paint onto paper. Why not make a collection. Here are some ideas to start you off:

Corrugated card, bubble pack, corks, cotton reels, sponges, cotton wadding, jars with the labels still on, leaves, cut fruit and vegetables, off-cuts of wood, cloth, old shoes, boxes, etc.

cloths

decorating brushes

paint-brushes

toothbrush

nail-brush

scrubbing brush

shaving brush

9

Colour Mixing

What colour will it make? All you will need is a basic set of paints (see page 7), a white plate and a brush to find out!

Mix red and yellow to make orange. Add more red for a warmer orange and more yellow for a tangerine shade.

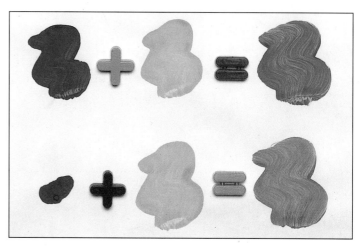

Blue and yellow mixed together makes green. You can vary the shade by adding more or less yellow or blue.

Mix a brushful of red with a drop of blue. Now try a drop of red with a brushful of blue. How is it different?

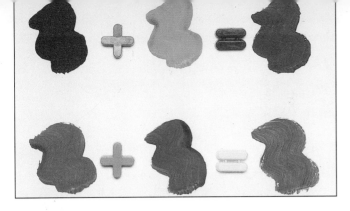

Red and green mixed together makes brown. Now try orange and blue.

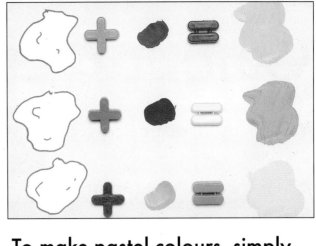

To make pastel colours, simply add a drop of any coloured paint to white paint.

Now see what happens when you mix a drop of black to any colour.

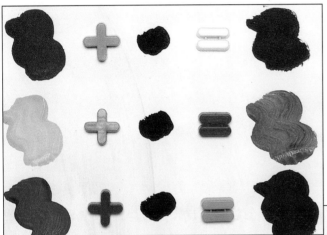

Skin tones are harder to mix. Here are a couple of examples. Now try to mix a colour to match your skin.

Sqeeze small amounts of paint onto an old saucer or plate, or even a thick piece of card. Use a brush to mix them together.

What an Effect

Have a go at using some of the tools on pages 8 and 9 to explore these painting techniques.

Dry Brush

Put a little paint onto the tip of a dry brush and work it into the bristles by brushing lightly on newspaper. Now paint onto paper – try adding other colours.

Stippling

Cut out a shape from paper and place onto a sheet of card. Dab around the edges of the cut-out shape with a lightly-painted brush.

Rolling and combing

1 Roll a thick layer of paint onto a sheet of card. If you do not have a roller, use a jar with the label still on it.

2 Make a comb by cutting teeth along one edge of a square of thick card. Drag and twist the comb through the paint.

Splattering

Dip a toothbrush into some watered-down paint. Run a paint-brush handle along its bristles to splatter the paint onto the paper. What effect will you get with a nail-brush?

Newspaper Crumple

Screw a piece of newspaper into a crumpled ball. Dab into paint and print onto paper. Use other balls of crumpled paper to add more colours.

IN THE FRAME

Frame your pictures as you paint them. Cut two L-shaped pieces of thick card. Position these onto the paper so that they mark off a rectangular area. Paint within this area and then remove the card pieces for an instant frame.

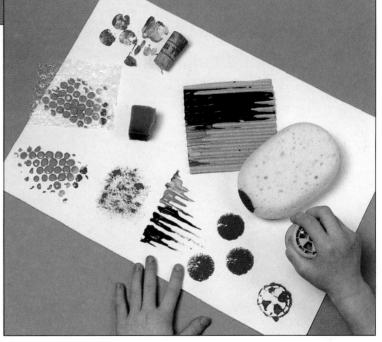

You can use all sorts of things collected from around the house to paint with. Now see what you can find.

The Background Story

Why use only plain paper to draw or paint on when you can create an interesting textured background?

Streaking and dripping

Dip a middle-sized decorating brush into watered-down paint and hold the brush at the top of the paper. Lift the paper and let the paint drip down.

Washes

Dip a large decorating brush into watered-down paint and brush across the paper. Now add different coloured washes, letting the colours run into each other.

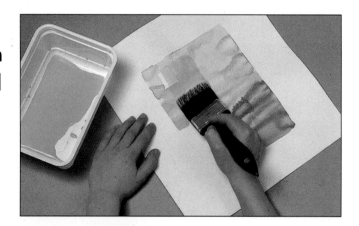

Tonking

1 Paint thickly onto a sheet of paper. Cover an area of the painted paper with newspaper and flatten with your hand.

2 Carefully lift off the newspaper.

Rag Rolling

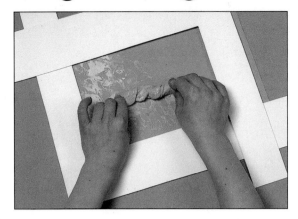

1 Put a rag into a tray of paint and stir until it is well covered. Gather into a wrinkled sausage. Place at the bottom left-hand corner of the paper and roll up.

2 Continue to roll the rag in columns across the paper. If the rag print becomes faint, dip the rag in paint again.

Staining

!1 You can use all sorts of household products to stain white paper, for example shoe polish, turmeric, vinegar, coffee, food colouring and soya sauce. Make up a sample sheet like the one in the photograph.

2 Choose your favourite one and stain some sheets of white paper for future paintings. This tea wash is used as a background for the next project in this book.

Me! Me! Me!

A good place to start painting is with a portrait of yourself.

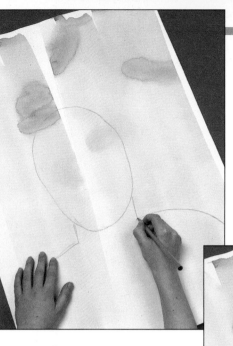

1 Take a textured sheet of paper. Sit in front of a mirror and look at the shape of your face. Draw the outline of it in the centre of the paper.

2 Divide the face up into quarters by marking in light pencil lines horizontally and vertically.

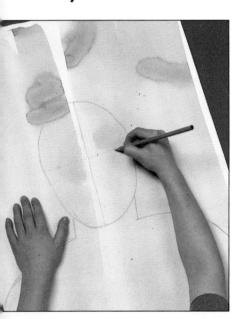

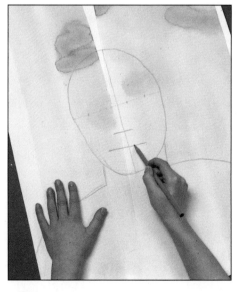

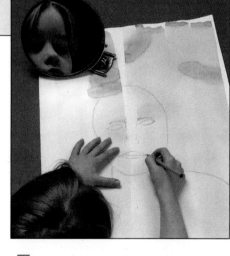

3 Divide the horizontal or eyeline into fifths, to give you a guide for positioning the corners of the eyes.

4 Mark in lines for the nose and mouth on the bottom half of the vertical line.

5 Look at your face again. Use the pencil guidelines to help you draw what you see. Rub out these lines when you are happy with your drawing.

16

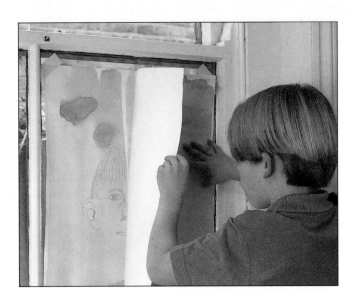

6 Before beginning to paint over your drawing make a copy of it. Tape it onto a window and place a sheet of paper on top of it. Trace off your drawing.

7 Paint over your original drawing. Try to match the colour of your eyes and hair. Mark in any freckles. Don't forget your eyebrows and eyelashes.

Trace copies from your original to make countless versions of yourself.

Fruit and Vegetable Printing

Instead of painting a still life of a bowl of fruit, use the fruit (and some vegetables too) to paint the picture!

[!] 1 Ask your mum or dad if you can have a selection of fruit and vegetables to paint with.

[!] 2 Now ask your parent if he or she could cut up the fruit and vegetables so that you can print with them.

3 Put out the colours you will need onto a plate. Paint the cut end of a vegetable and begin to print a border around a large sheet of paper.

4 The painted edge of a carrot stick has been used to print this bowl and the table mat beneath it.

5 An apple cut in half and painted has been used to print different coloured apples in the bowl.

6 The round end of a carrot has been used to build up a bunch of grapes. A half a lemon has been used to print an orange. The round end of a carrot painted red makes the cherries.

You can have great fun experimenting with the variety of effects that can be achieved with this simple printing technique.

Tree of Life Stencil

A stencil is made by cutting a pattern from a piece of card or paper. It can then be painted over to reproduce the same pattern as many times as you like.

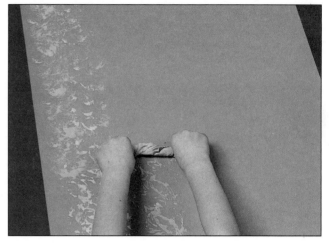

1 Rag roll over a sheet of paper using a slightly lighter shade of paint than the colour of the paper. Leave to dry.

2 To make the trunk and branches of the tree, paint your hand and forearm brown and print at the bottom of the paper.

3 Draw half shapes of leaves, butterflies, hearts, flowers and stars along the folded line of some small squares of white paper. Cut out the shapes and open up the paper. These are your stencils.

4 Put a stencil on the ragged paper. Stipple the paint all over the stencil. Take care that the paint does not creep under the edge of the stencil.

5 Fill out the shape of the tree by building up a pattern of stencils across the paper. Leave to dry.

The finished picture. Now make several versions. Cut more stencils – try varying the shapes of the leaves.

6 To add some detail to your picture, cut a leaf vein stencil from paper. Place the stencil over the painted leaves and stipple with black paint.

Draw With Glue

A picture drawn with glue makes a wonderful printing block.

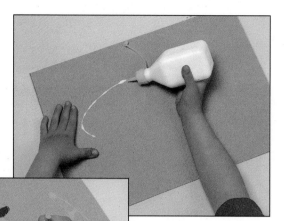

1 Use glue to draw a picture onto a piece of thick card. Leave to dry overnight.

2 When the glue has dried completely, colour in the areas between the lines with wax or oil-based crayons.

3 Paint all over the surface of the card. Work fast so that the paint does not dry.

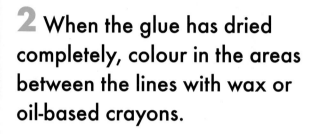

4 Lay a sheet of white tissue-paper over the painted card and smooth down with your hands. Carefully peel back the tissue-paper.

5 Put the tissue-paper print to one side to dry.

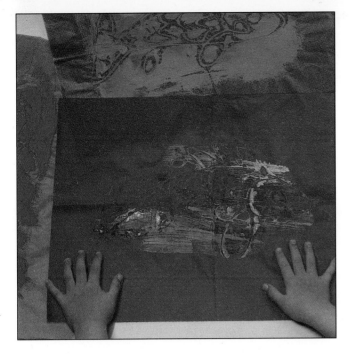

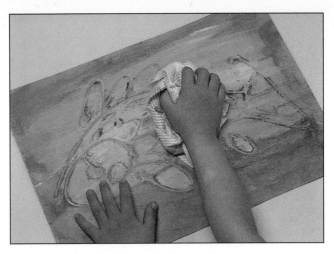

6 Paint all over the card again. This time make a print onto a coloured sheet of tissue-paper. You can make as many prints of your picture as you like.

7 When you have made all the prints you want, use a damp cloth to wipe most of the paint off the card. Leave some paint in the corners. When you have finished, the colour of the crayons should be showing through brightly again.

The printing card has become a picture in itself. Make a frame for it and hang it on the wall.

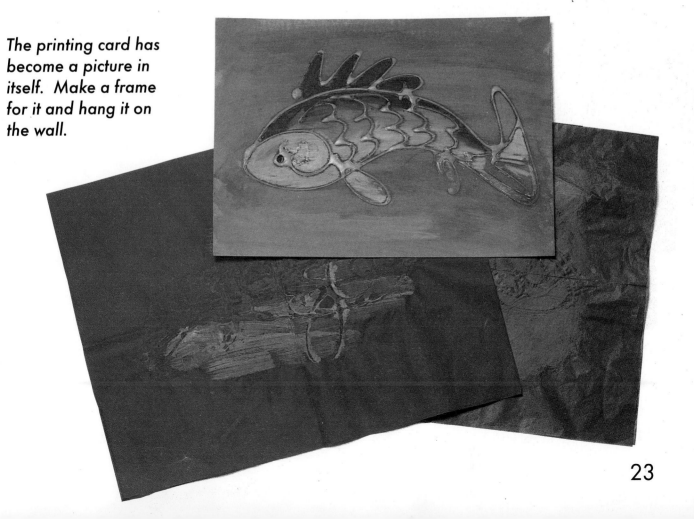

Cloth Printing

Transform an old sheet with a little paint and a simple printing block made from card.

! **1** Cut out a variety of shapes from thick card.

2 Arrange the cut shapes into a pattern on a square of thick card and glue in position. Make several printing blocks and leave to dry overnight.

! **3** Cut out a 60 cm x 60 cm square of cloth, iron and place on a bed of newspaper (6–8 layers) ready for printing onto. Quickly apply a thick layer of paint to a printing block.

4 Press the block down hard on the bottom edge of the cloth. Print another square next to the first, and so on.

Materials

newspapers

thick card

cloth

24

! 5 As the print fades, put more paint on the block. Build up a pyramid of printed squares. When the paint has dried, place the cloth upside down on the newspaper and iron.

! 6 Prepare another piece of cloth. Paint two printing blocks different colours and use in turn to print rows of squares.

7 To make table mats, cut out the printed squares. Make a fringe by pulling out the threads along the edges of the cloth.

Ask an adult to help you sew together two pieces of printed cloth to make a cushion cover.

FABRIC PAINTS
If you use ordinary paint for printing, the things you make from the printed cloth will not be washable. You can buy special fabric paints from an art shop that can be washed. These are used in exactly the same way.

String Pictures

In this project you will use string to draw with, print with and to make a decorative frame.

Materials

shells

string

thick card

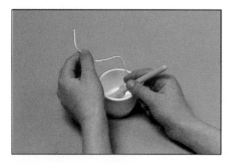

1 Put a long piece of string into a cupful of glue and stir it around.

2 Take the string out of the glue and pull it through your fingers so that it does not drip everywhere.

3 Lay the string on top of a small square of card (12 cm x 12 cm) to make a picture. You may need to cut the string into small pieces. Leave your string picture to dry overnight.

4 Lay paper onto a bed of newspaper. Paint over the string picture and press down hard onto the paper. Make several prints.

26

5 Choose your favourite print and frame it. Put the string picture in the centre of a large square of card (17 cm x 17 cm), draw around it and lift it off.

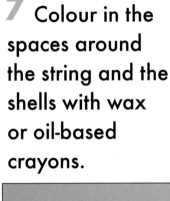

6 Decorate the border by drawing on a pattern with glue-covered string. Stick on some shells. Leave overnight to dry.

7 Colour in the spaces around the string and the shells with wax or oil-based crayons.

8 To give the frame an antique effect, paint all over the card with brown paint. Use a rag to dab off some of the paint.

Cut a print down to fit into the centre of the frame. Glue into place. Ask an adult to hang it up for you.

27

Painter's Sketchbook

Make this book to keep your favourite pictures in.

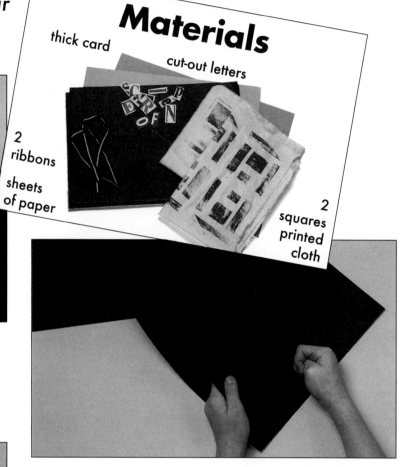

Materials

thick card

cut-out letters

2 ribbons

sheets of paper

2 squares printed cloth

1 Make a long strip of paper by gluing several sheets of paper end to end.

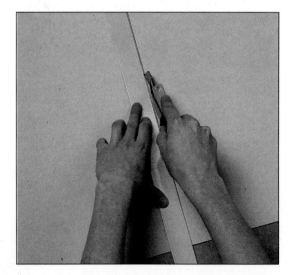

2 Fold evenly into a zig zag.

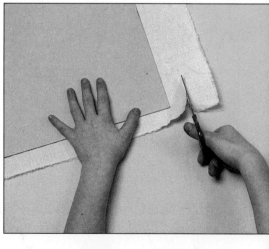

!3 Cut 2 pieces of thick card about 1 cm larger all around than the folded zig zag of paper.

4 Now cover both pieces of card with the printed cloth made on page 24.

Place the card on the cloth. Cut around the fabric leaving a 2.5 cm edge.

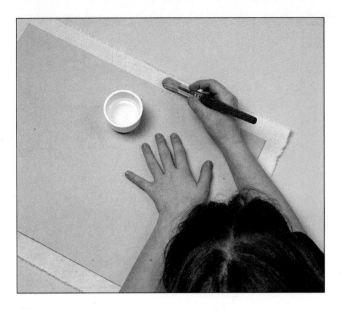

5 Use a brush to dampen the edges of the cloth with water.

6 Run a line of glue all around the edge of the cloth and a blob on each corner of the card.

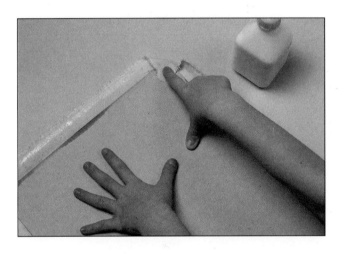

7 Fold the corners of the cloth over onto the card as shown.

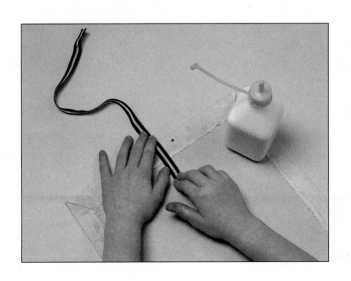

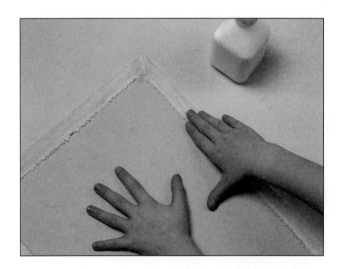

8 Fold over the sides of the cloth as shown. Make sure that the corner seams do not overlap each other, and check that the fabric is pulled tight across the front of the card.

9 Glue a length of ribbon onto each piece of card.

Continues on next page

10 Evenly spread a thin layer of glue over both pieces of card.

11 Run a thin line of glue close to the edge of the first page of the zig zag strip of paper. Press the paper onto a piece of covered card.

12 Glue around the last page of the zig zag strip and press onto the second piece of covered card. Make sure that the ribbons are both on the same side so they can be tied together.

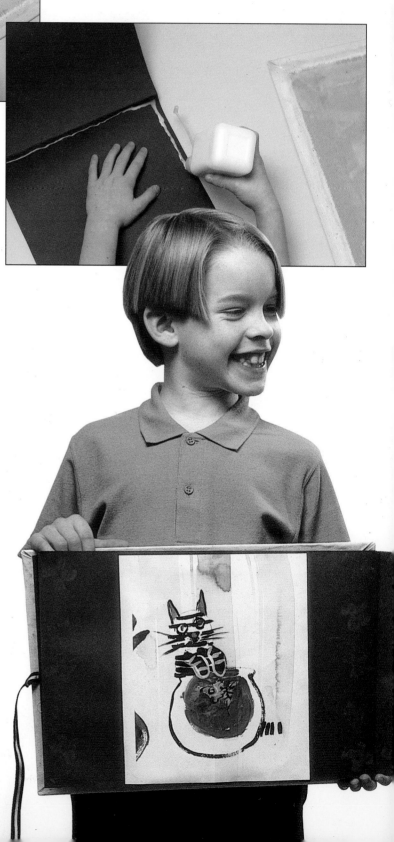

14 Cut out letters from magazine or newspaper headlines and make a title for your book.

13 Once the glue has dried (leave overnight) open up the concertina book and print a border around each page using a cut potato.

Fill your book with your favourite pictures painted by you, your family and your friends. When it is full, make a present of it to a friend.

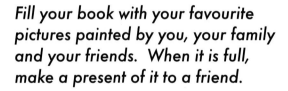

Fresco

Paint a picture onto the plaster surface of a small sheet of plasterboard and hang it on the wall. Plasterboard is cheap and can be bought from any DIY shop.

1 Use a large decorating brush to cover both sides of the plasterboard with water. Leave overnight to dry.

2 Mark out a large rectangle on the front of the board leaving an even frame all around.

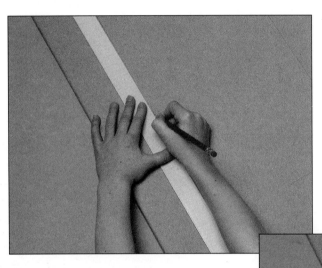

[!] **3** Ask an adult to cut through the paper along the marked lines just into the plaster below.

4 Carefully peel back the paper to reveal the plaster below. If the paper does not come away cleanly, run a wet paint-brush under the edge.

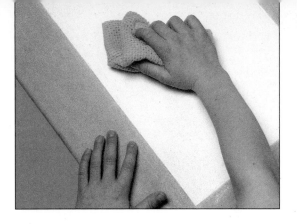

5 Scrub the plaster with a damp cloth. Scrap off any remaining patches of paper with a round-ended knife. Don't worry if the surface of the plaster looks scratched or pitted. This will give a more interesting effect when painted over.

6 Paint a picture onto the plaster using watered-down paint. Try a portrait of your mum or dad, or your pet.

7 Use stencils cut from thin card to decorate the paper frame. Use a thick brush to stipple the paint onto the stencil, taking care not to let paint creep under the edge.

Furniture Painting

An old piece of furniture can be transformed by your imagination and just a little paint. But do ask mum or dad for permission first.

1 Use fine sandpaper to rub down the area of wood to be painted.

2 Put a little washing-up liquid into a bowl of warm water and wash down the sanded wood. Leave to dry.

3 Sketch out a rough design for the area to be painted. This is just a guide, and you can change it as you work.

4 Cut all the stencils you will need from thin card.

34

5 Work outwards from the centre of your design. Tape the stencil to the wood.

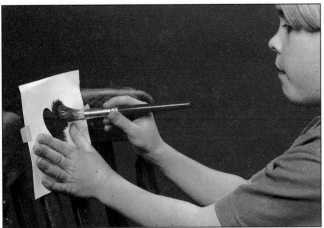

6 Use a thick brush to dab paint over the stencil.

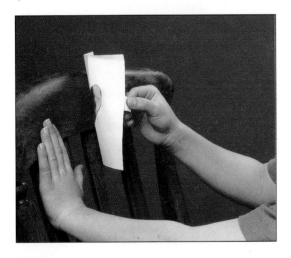

! **7** Carefully peel off the stencil. Build up your design using one stencil at a time. Once the paint has dried ask an adult to help you brush the painted area with a thin coat of varnish.

The finished chair. Now everyone will want to sit on it.

35

Printing & Stencilling

Before beginning the projects in this section, it is a good idea to collect together some tools first. You will need a roller to roll paint out and a flat surface to roll it on to (see page 38). Card and string come in useful for making blocks to print with and you will need a stencil brush and sponge for stencilling. Other useful tools are pictured here.

flat inking surface

round-ended knife

roller

scissors

masking tape

paint-brushes

paints

Paint

Water-based paints and printing inks are used for many of the projects in this section. You can use whichever you prefer. Buy the paint ready-mixed in large, easy-to-use, squeezy bottles. The printing inks come in tubes. The basic colours you will need are red, yellow, blue, black and white. From these you can mix all other colours. The paints and inks can be thinned by adding water to them.

Oil paints, fabric paints, fabric dyes and food colouring are also used and more information is given about these on page 96.

spoon

Other Useful Things

Almost anything with a raised surface can be used for printing with, so do keep a look out for useful things around the home.

Here are some ideas:

Corrugated card, bubble pack, corks, cotton reels, cardboard tubes, cut fruit and vegetables, leaves, buttons, off-cuts of wood, cloth, old shoes, keys, bottle tops, spent matches, shaped biscuit cutters.

tracing paper

metal ruler

string

pencil and eraser

paper

craft knife

oil pastels or wax crayons

felt-tip pens

ruler

printing inks

glue

tissue-paper

sponge

stencil brush

thick and thin card

Remember

☆ Wear an apron and cover the work area.
☆ Collect together the items in the materials box at the beginning of each project.
☆ Always ask an adult for help when you see this sign [!]
☆ Clear up after yourself.

Keep on Rolling

For many of the projects in this book you will need to roll out the printing ink or paint before you begin work. For this you will need a roller and a smooth flat surface such as an off-cut of plastic laminate, or you could use the shiny side of a piece of hardboard or a piece of thick polythene sheeting.

Rolling Out

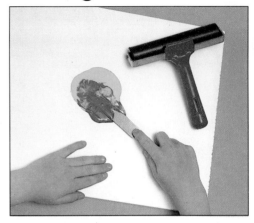

1 Put the paint on to the flat surface. Use a small round-ended knife to mix colours together.

2 Use a roller to roll out the mixed paint in all directions until there is an even layer of paint all over the surface.

3 You can now use the roller to transfer the paint on to a printing block ready to print.

Here are 2 ways to make a print directly from rolled out paint or ink. Roll out very thinly and work quickly as the ink dries very fast.

Transfer Print

1 When the rolled out ink is nearly dry, lay a piece of coloured paper on to it and put one of your drawings on top. Firmly go over the drawing with a coloured pencil.

2 When you peel the coloured sheet off the inked surface you will see that you have made a print of your drawing.

Paper Resist

1 Fold a piece of paper in half and cut a square from the folded edge. Open out and lay on to the rolled out ink. Cut out paper shapes and lay them on to the inked surface to make a picture.

Lightly dampen a sheet of paper and lay on top of the paper shapes.

2 Run a clean roller all over the back of the paper, and carefully lift off to reveal the print.

Letters and Numbers

With just 4 shapes cut from a potato you can print the whole alphabet and any number too.

1 Trace the 4 shapes on page 94 on to card and cut out.

2 Cut a large potato into slabs about 1 cm thick. Draw around the card shapes on to the potato slabs and cut out.

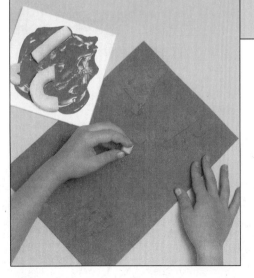

3 Use a round-ended knife to mix and spread an even area of paint on to a flat surface.

4 Dip the potato shapes into the paint and try printing some letters.

MAKE A NAME PLAQUE

You can use the shapes to print out your name on to a piece of card. Why not print a border too. When the plaque is finished punch 2 holes at the top and thread through some ribbon so that you can hang it up on your bedroom door.

To print a border around the plaque, cut the end of a carrot into a heart shape. ⚠

5 Now try to print some numbers with your potato shapes.

This alphabet sampler shows you how to make all the letters of the alphabet with your potato shapes.

Bricks and Paper

This is the house that you built. . . from a small cardboard box!

Bricks and Tiles

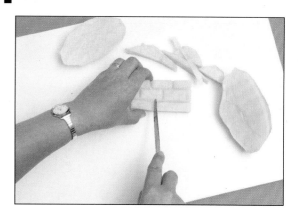

[!] 1 Ask an adult to cut a peeled potato into a 2-cm thick slab measuring about 3.5 cm x 7 cm. Cut thin grooves into the potato to look like bricks.

2 Dip the potato into red-brown paint and use it to print lines on to white paper.

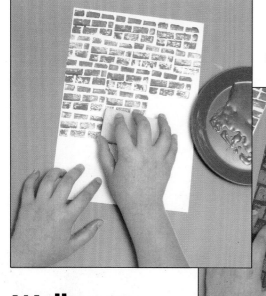

[!] 3 To make roof tiles, cut square-shaped grooves into a potato slab and use to print dark brown paint on to black paper.

Wallpaper

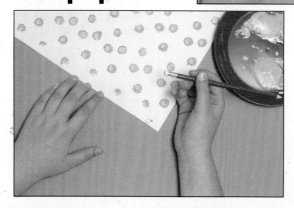

[!] 4 Ask an adult to cut a flower shape from the end of a carrot and use it to print all over a large sheet of paper. Add some colour to the centre of the flower heads with a pencil-top eraser.

[!] 5 Make a leaf stamp and use to print leaves at the base of the flower heads.

42

The House

6 To make a support to hold a roof cut 2 card triangles and tape to the front and back of the top of the house.

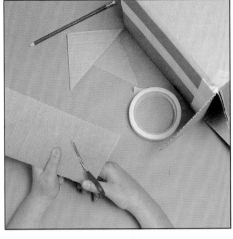

NOTE: The base of each triangle should be as wide as the side of the box.

7 Cut a rectangle of card to fit snugly between the 2 triangular supports and tape in place. Cover the box with the brick paper.

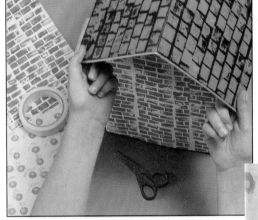

8 Cover a large piece of corrugated card with roof tile paper. Fold in half and tape to the roof supports.

To finish off the house paint the inside walls or cover them with the printed wallpaper. Make a 2-storey house by taping a piece of card in the middle of the box.

43

Wax Wonder

Make a beautiful rainbow-coloured print of one of your favourite drawings

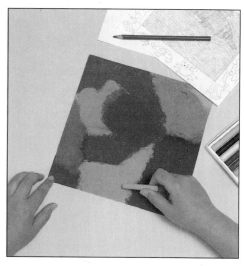

1 Cover a sheet of paper all over with oil pastels or wax crayons. Use bright colours, but avoid yellow as it does not transfer very well.

2 Put a clean sheet of paper on to the crayoned sheet, then put your drawing on top.

Make sure the edges of all 3 sheets of paper are lined up and keep together with paper clips.

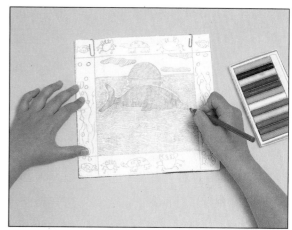

3 Go over your drawing with a coloured pencil, pressing firmly. This will transfer your drawing in colour on to the middle sheet of paper.

You can make as many prints as you like from your drawing, but do re-wax the crayoned sheet each time.

Mirror Image

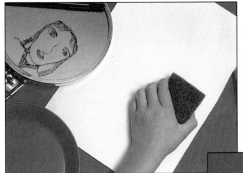

A simple way to make a print of your face.

2 Lightly sponge a piece of paper to dampen it. Place the damp side on to the mirror and smooth flat all over.

1 Sit in front of a mirror. Close one eye. Use a washable fibre-tip pen to draw around your mirror image.

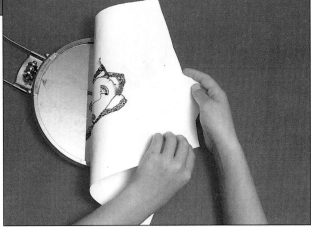

3 Lift off the paper to reveal your self-portrait.

This is the perfect way to draw a picture of yourself, but do make sure that you use a washable fibre-tip pen.

45

Fish in a Net

Make a simple printing block from corrugated card to print the fish and a roller from a cardboard tube and a piece of string to print the net.

1 Trace the large fish template on page 94 on to corrugated card and cut out.

2 Roll paint across the fish and use it to print on to coloured paper.

! **3** To make a stamp to print the scales on to the fish, ask an adult to cut away half of the end of a cork to make a semi-circle.

4 Use the rim of a bottle top to print the eye. Use a pencil-top eraser dipped into paint to print the centre of the eye.

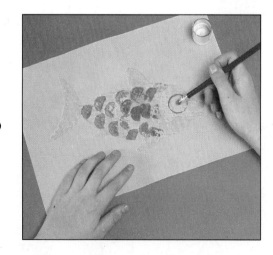

5 Print the small fish with a shaped biscuit cutter. Alternatively, trace the template on page 94 on to card, cut out and use it to print with.

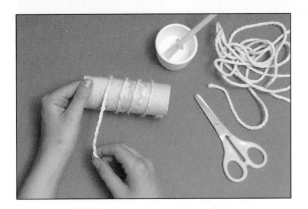

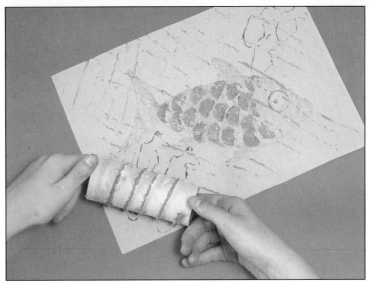

6 Glue string in a spiral around a cardboard tube.

Glue the finished picture in the centre of a large piece of coloured card. You could decorate the card frame with stencilled starfish and shells.

7 Roll the tube in paint until the string is completely covered. Roll diagonally over your picture both ways.

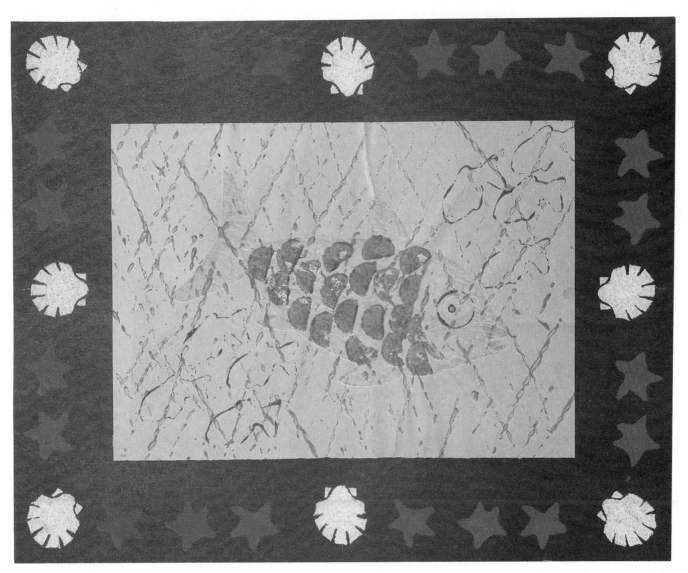

Surprise Tree

A cat and a bird are hidden amongst the branches of this tree printing block. There are templates for the cat and bird on page 94, but have a go at making the tree yourself.

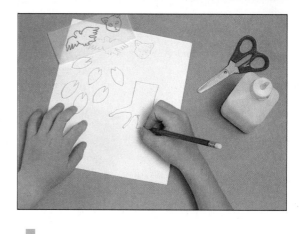

1 Trace the cat and bird templates on page 94 on to thin card. Now draw a tree trunk and leaf shapes on to the thin card. Cut out all the shapes.

2 To make a frame glue 1-cm wide strips of card around the edges of a thick piece of card measuring 21 x 29.5 cm. Glue on the cut card shapes to make a tree picture. Leave to dry.

3 First make a rubbing of the finished picture. Put a piece of paper on top of the card and rub a wax crayon across the surface.

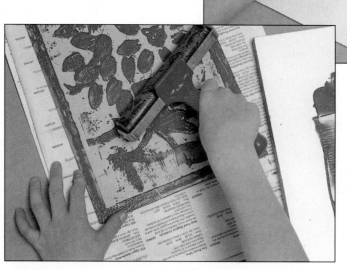

4 Now make a print. Roll paint all over the surface of the printing block.

5 Lay a piece of paper the same size as the printing block on top of it and carefully line up the edges. Rub firmly all over with the back of a spoon.

⚠ 6 Cut the end off a carrot to make a small circle. Dip in red paint and use it to print cherries all over the tree.

For a really special effect why not print over the cat and bird shape once again, but this time dip the cat and bird printing blocks in gold poster paint first.

7 Cut another cat and bird shape from thin card and glue on to the end of 2 corks. Dip into paint and use to print over the cat and bird shape in the branches of the tree.

Printing Press

You can make a printing block from polystyrene food packaging. Wash it well first.

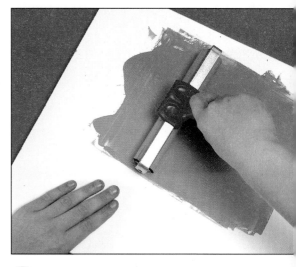

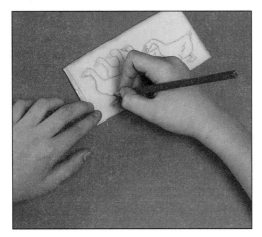

1 Make a tracing of a favourite picture. Tape the tracing to a piece of polystyrene cut to size. To transfer the drawing to the polystyrene, firmly go over it with a blunt, coloured pencil.

2 Roll out the printing ink on to a flat surface (see page 38). For a colour blend try rolling out 2 colours side by side, mixing a bit in the centre, then rolling backwards and forwards only.

3 Roll the printing ink across the polystyrene printing block once.

4 Centre the polystyrene printing block on to a piece of paper and press down firmly.

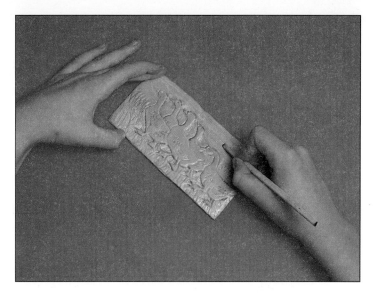

5 The paper will stick to the ink. Turn it over and rub firmly all over the paper with the back of a spoon to get an even print. Carefully lift off the polystyrene. Wash the polystyrene, roller and inking surface.

6 To add another colour to the picture, use a stick to press into the bits of the printing block that you do not want to print again.

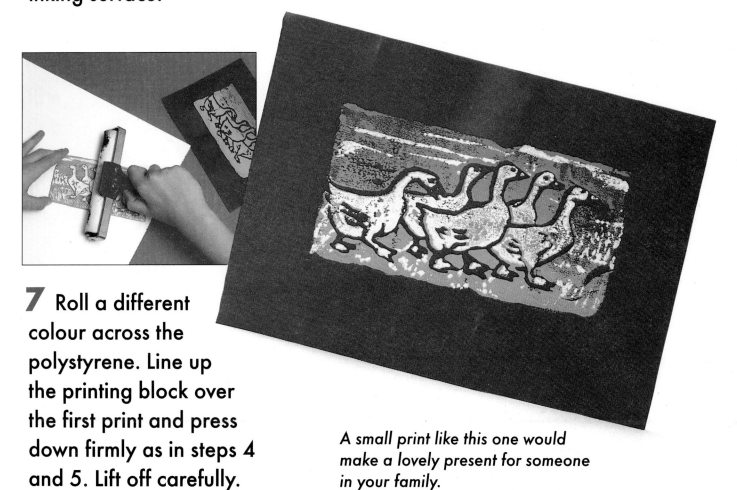

7 Roll a different colour across the polystyrene. Line up the printing block over the first print and press down firmly as in steps 4 and 5. Lift off carefully.

A small print like this one would make a lovely present for someone in your family.

Circus Wagons

Print a circus wagon frieze for your bedroom wall.

1 Fold an A4 sheet of paper in half and cut a rectangle from the folded edge. Open and place on another piece of A4 paper lining up the edges. Sponge paint all over the inside of the cut rectangle and leave to dry.

2 Trace the lion template on page 95 on to thick paper and cut out to make a stencil. Place the lion stencil in the centre of the sponged rectangle.

3 Dip a stencil brush into paint. Dab the brush up and down all over the inside of the stencil taking care that the paint does not seep under the edges.

4 Print the edges of the wagon using strips cut from corrugated cardboard.

5 Use a cut cork and carrot to print the top of the wagon. Print on the wheels with the cut carrot. Use a pencil-top eraser to add the finishing touches.

52

6 Cut a stencil for the lion's mane (template page 95). Carefully line up on the lion's head and stencil with dark brown paint.

7 Use the edge of a piece of thick card to print the cage bars.

Use the leopard and giraffe templates on page 95 to make more circus wagons. Glue the printed wagons on to thin card and cut out. Join together the 3 wagons with bits of string and stick to a piece of black card.

Balancing Butterfly

Amaze your friends by effortlessly balancing this butterfly on the end of a pencil.

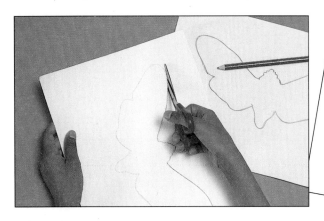

Materials

objects to print with

2 nuts

thin card

1 To make a stencil trace the butterfly on page 94 on to paper and cut out.

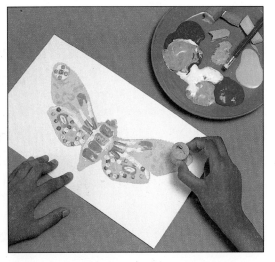

2 Place the stencil on to thin card and sponge print. Leave to dry.

3 Decorate the butterfly by printing all over it with cut vegetables, cut card, erasers or any other objects dipped into paint.

4 When the butterfly is dry, cut it out.

5 Glue the nuts to the top corners of the back of the wings.

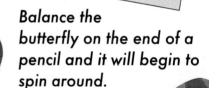

BLOT BUTTERFLIES
Draw half a butterfly along the folded edge of a piece of paper. Cut out and open flat. Drop blobs of paint on to one half of the butterfly, fold over and press firmly. Open and leave to dry.

Balance the butterfly on the end of a pencil and it will begin to spin around.

What a colourful display. The blot butterflies on the right are very easy to make.

Dino Print

Bring new life to an old T-shirt with this fantastic dinosaur stencil. All you need are fabric paints.

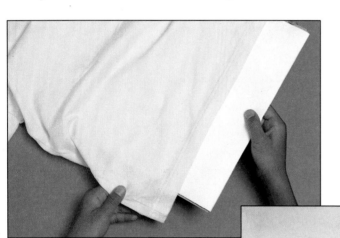

1 Trace the dinosaur and footprint templates on page 95 on to thin card and cut out to make the stencils.

2 Put a piece of card, covered with blotting paper, inside a washed and ironed T-shirt.

3 Tape the stencil in the centre of the T-shirt. Mask off the rest of the T-shirt by taping paper all around the stencil. Dip a stiff brush into the fabric paint. Test on paper first, and then with a dabbing up and down motion paint all over the stencil.

4 Remove the paper and carefully lift off the stencil. Leave to dry.

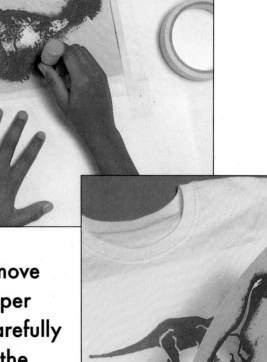

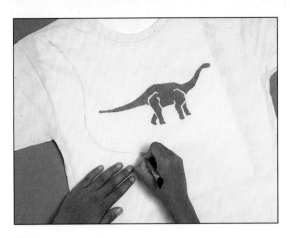

5 Use tailor's chalk to mark on the trail of footprints.

7 Use a small brush to add the 3 toe markings to finish off each footprint.

6 Stencil the footprints along the marked trail. Protect the T-shirt from paint splashes by laying a large piece of paper that has had a rectangle cut from the middle of it over the footprint stencil.

The finished T-shirt.

! **8** To fix the fabric paint, cover the stencilled area with a clean cloth, and press with a hot iron for 2 minutes.

Japanese Paper Fold

All you need to make this printed paper is paper, food colouring and a rubber band. But it is worth remembering that the thinner the paper you use, the easier it will be to fold.

1 Fold over the edge of the paper by 2 cm and press down. Turn over

and fold over by 2 cm again. Repeat until all the paper has been folded.

2 Holding the paper fan together, fold the bottom right corner to the left edge to make a triangle.

3 Turn over and fold the triangle straight up, pressing firmly with your fingertips.

4 Turn over and fold the bottom left corner to the right edge to make a triangle.

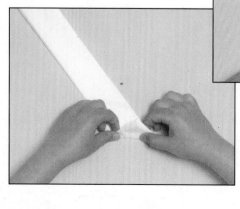

5 Turn over and fold the triangle straight up, pressing firmly once again.

58

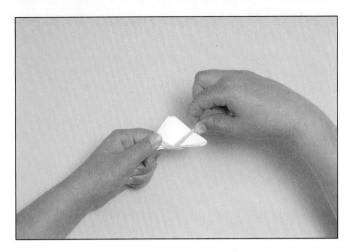

6 Continue folding as in steps 2 to 5 until you reach the top of the paper. Finish with a triangle fold. To hold the folded paper triangle together, put the rubber band around one corner, twist it and loop over the opposite corner.

7 Put undiluted food colouring into three small dishes. Dip each edge of the folded paper triangle into a different colour, leaving the centre white.

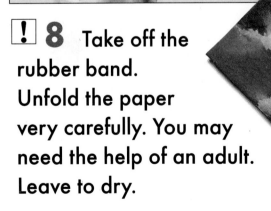

⚠ 8 Take off the rubber band. Unfold the paper very carefully. You may need the help of an adult. Leave to dry.

The finished paper makes beautiful gift wrapping. Or try taping a tissue-paper sheet to a window for a stained glass effect.

Tie and Dye

Have fun with this traditional way of printing patterns on to fabric.

Circles

1 Pick up a fabric square in the centre and tie firmly in 3 places with string that has been waxed with a candle.

Marble

Scrunch up a fabric square and tie with waxed string, criss crossing the string over itself many times. Follow steps 2-4.

Tile Squares

Fold the fabric square up into a small square. Sandwich the folded fabric between 2 blocks of wood and tie tightly. Follow steps 2-4.

2 Place in the dye, and leave for 15 to 60 minutes following the fabric dye manufacturer's instructions.

How you tie the fabric before dying can produce very different results.

Beans

Lightly pencil a pattern of dots on to a fabric square. Centre a bean on each pencil dot and tie in place with waxed string. Follow steps 2-4.

60

3 Use a pair of tongs or a fork to lift out the fabric from the dye,

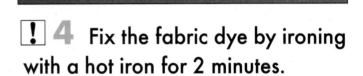

and rinse under cold water. Untie the string. Open out the fabric and leave to dry.

Broad Stripe

Fold over the edge of the fabric square by 2 cm. Turn over and fold over by 2 cm again. Repeat until all the fabric has been folded into a fan. Tie broad stripes of waxed string at intervals along the folded fabric. Dye and rinse. Undo some of the string to the original colour. Tie more string around the freshly dyed areas and then dip into a second colour dye. Follow steps 3-4.

! **4** Fix the fabric dye by ironing with a hot iron for 2 minutes.

Seven Colours

Follow the instructions for Broad Stripe. Now fold the dyed fabric square into a fan the opposite way. Tie with broad stripes of waxed string along the folded fabric and dip into a third colour dye. Follow steps 3-4.

Materials

white spirit

2 pots of oil paint

strips of newspaper

plastic tray

Plastic fork

1 litre of gelatine ⚠

printing paper

Marbling

To get the best results, you do need to use oil paints for marbling. These will stain, so do be careful.

⚠ **1** Squeeze 2 different colours of oil paint into separate containers. Mix white spirit into the oil paints to make them slightly runny.

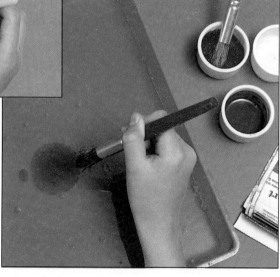

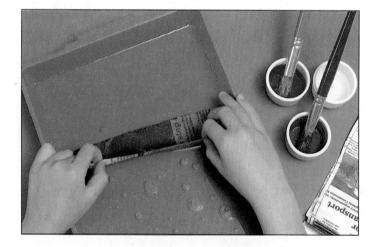

2 Pour the gelatine into the shallow tray and skim the surface with a strip of newspaper.

3 Shake a drop of the paint on to the skimmed surface. If the drop spreads into a circle larger than a milk bottle top it is too thin – add more paint. If the paint drops to the bottom of the tray, it is too thick – add a drop more white spirit.

5 Holding a piece of paper at opposite ends, lower it on to the surface of the gelatine and smooth to get rid of any air bubbles. Lift off and leave to dry. To make another piece of marbled paper, skim the surface with the newspaper strip and repeat from step 4.

Try dropping one colour inside the centre of another and watch it spread the first colour. Or use a comb to spread the paint across the skimmed surface.

4 When the consistency of the paint is just right, skim the surface with the newspaper strip again. Drop the 2 different colours on to the surface of the gelatine, and use a plastic fork to gently move the paint around to form patterns.

To make your own card stationery: dip only the edges of a piece of card into the tray.

Marbled paper can be used to cover tins, books, scrap books or for wrapping paper. To flatten the marbled paper leave it under a heavy book overnight.

Collage

In this section you will find out how to make pictures and objects by sticking all sorts of bits and pieces on to a background. That background might be paper, a box, a bottle or even an old plastic container. Before you begin the projects in this section it is a good idea to collect together some useful things first. A variety of different papers and glue are your basic tools (see page 66) but all sorts of other things will come in useful too.

double-sided
tape

pair of
compasses

pinking
shears

clear tape

scissors

masking
tape

paint-brushes

toothbrush

brown paper
tape

paint

Other Useful Things

All sorts of things come in useful for making collages. Start a collection and keep adding to it. Store useful odds and ends in a box. Your collection might include:

Cardboard tubes, plastic containers, glass bottles and jars, bottle tops, jar lids, old newspapers and magazines, corrugated cardboard, coloured card and coloured paper, gold and silver foil, gummed paper, crêpe paper, tissue-paper, wool, string, gold and silver thread, cellophane and sweet wrappers, glitter, confetti, stickers, buttons, sequins, felt, material off-cuts, ribbons, metal scraps, nuts and bolts.

metal ruler

graph paper

pencil and eraser

thick string

craft knife

bread knife

ruler

bradawl

wire cutters

hammer

Remember

☆ Wear an apron and cover the work area.
☆ Collect together the items in the materials box at the beginning of each project.
☆ Always ask an adult for help when you see this sign ❗
☆ Clear up after yourself.

Paper and Glue

You can make exciting collages using just paper and glue. It's a good idea to set aside a box to store different kinds of paper in. Keep a look out for different colours and textures. Save old magazines, wrapping papers, the labels off tins, used stamps, paper bags, newspapers, used envelopes, junk mail, and interesting cardboard boxes.

Wallpaper paste for papier mâché and making paper. You can paint and draw over this but it takes 24 hours to dry.

PVA is strong and quick drying. You can also use it to brush over your finished work to make it look shiny.

Glue stick won't wrinkle paper.

Tear and Cut

You can make an interesting collage by mixing shapes that you have carefully cut out together with shapes that you have torn from paper.

Tissue-paper Weave

1 Cut squares of different coloured tissue-paper and glue on to a piece of card. Cut strips of tissue-paper and stick over the squares.

2 Paste a few more tissue-paper squares on top of the strips. Paste PVA glue all over the finished picture to make it look shiny.

Nothing Wasted

Cut shapes from paper, such as circles, squares, rectangles, leaves and hearts. Make a picture by sticking the cut shapes and the paper they were cut from on to a piece of card.

Tiger! Tiger!

A simple collage of a bright, bouncing tiger made by gluing layers of tissue-paper on to card.

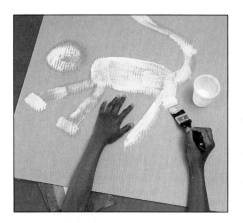

1 Use a large brushful of glue to paint the head and body of a tiger on to the cardboard sheet. Use more glue to paint on the legs and tail. You will need to work quickly before the glue dries.

2 Smooth 1 or 2 sheets of yellow tissue-paper over the glue-painted tiger. Leave to dry overnight.

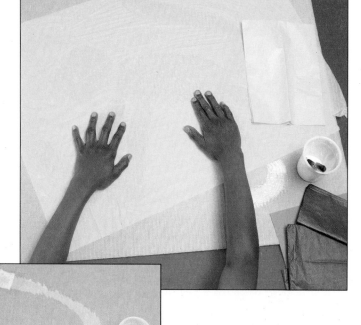

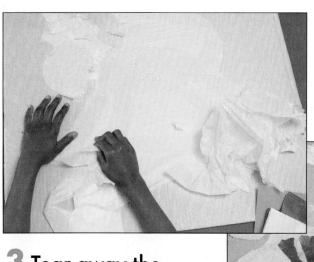

3 Tear away the unglued tissue-paper to leave the outline of the tiger.

4 Glue torn tissue-paper strips and shapes on to the tiger outline to add detail.

68

5 Now add some background detail, but keep it simple so that the tiger stands out – a yellow semi-circle for the sun, blue strips for the sky and green and yellow strips for the grass.

The finished picture. When you are adding detail to the tiger outline in step 4, it might help if you copy a picture of a tiger from a book.

When adding the black and white stripes, don't worry if they come off the edge of the tiger. This will give a feeling of movement.

To make the frame see page 70.

Frame Up

All you need to make this frame is one side of a cardboard box. If the picture to be framed is very large like this one, you'll need a very large cardboard box.

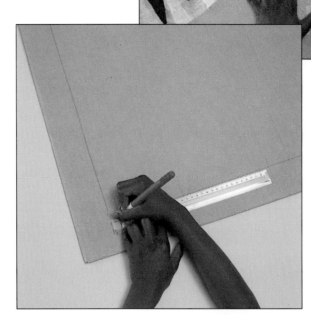

1 Cut a piece of cardboard exactly the same size as your picture.

[!] **2** Rule a line along each side of the cardboard 6 cm from the edge. Ask an adult to cut out the marked off area in the middle to make a frame.

3 The piece of card cut from the centre of the frame is used to decorate it. Cut the card into strips, squares and triangles that will fit along the edge of the frame.

4 Use the cut cardboard shapes to make a pattern along the frame and glue them in place. Paint and leave to dry.

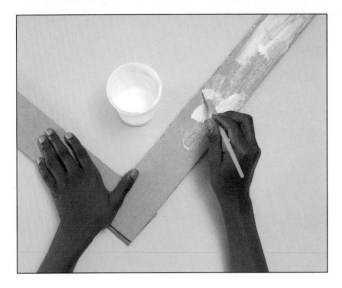

5 Brush glue all the way around the edge of the back of the frame. Put the picture front side down on to the glue, press around the edges firmly and leave to dry.

6 Make a hole in the top 2 corners of the frame. Thread about 1 metre of thick string through the holes and tie a knot at each end.

Ask your mum or dad to help you find a place to hang up your pictures so that everyone can admire them.

A. B. The Robot

Metal jar lids, broken chains and discarded keys will all come in useful to make this collage.

TIP BOX [!]
Use a hammer to flatten bottle and jar lids and old tin cans to use in your metal collage. The best place to do this is outside on cement.

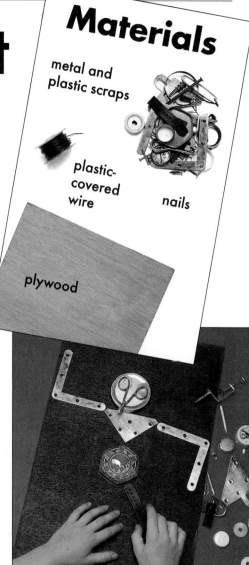

Materials

metal and plastic scraps

plastic-covered wire

nails

plywood

1 Paint the plyboard black on one side.

2 Arrange the metal and plastic scraps on to the painted board to make a picture of a robot.

3 Once you have made a picture that you are happy with, glue the metal and plastic bits in place with strong glue.

4 [!] You can also use screws to secure the metal scraps, or hammer them in place with carpet tacks.

5 !! To make a frame for your picture, hammer 2-3 nails along each side of the plyboard.

6 Wind plastic-covered wire several times around the nail frame.

Why not make up a story about your robot. This one's called Auntie Barbara and she babysits for tool boxes.

Materials

4 small cardboard tubes

pink tissue-paper

newspaper

printed wrapping paper

newspaper strips

plastic container

Pig Bank

This money box is made by covering a used plastic container with papier mâché, and then decorating it with tissue-paper and a collage of cut-out pictures.

⚠️ **1** Wash the plastic container well in warm soapy water and leave to dry. Ask an adult to cut off the handle.

2 To make the pig's legs, cut tabs two-thirds the way around one end of the cardboard tubes. Bend back the tabs and tape a cardboard roll to each corner of the plastic container.

3 Brush the pig with wallpaper paste and lay on

newspaper strips crossing them over each other as you go. Continue in this way until the pig is completely covered (apart from its nose).

4 Cover the pig with at least 3 layers of papier mâché. Where the legs join the body add extra strips for a strong join.

5 To make each ear tear a few pieces of newspaper roughly the same size. Brush with paste and place on top of each other. Fold to a point at one corner.

6 To make a tail, twist together several strips of pasted newspaper.

7 Paste the ears and tail in place. Cover the joins with strips of pasted newspaper as in step 4. Leave the pig to dry in a warm dry place for at least 24 hours.

Once the pig has dried out completely you can decorate it. Paint it pink or cover it with several layers of pink tissue-paper. Stick pictures cut from printed wrapping papers all over it. Finally, ask an adult to cut a slit along the pig bank's back so that you can post through your money. To get the money out again, unscrew the pig's nose.

Salt Bottles

Materials

glitter

air hardening modelling clay

picture scraps

salt

bottle or jar

This is a great way to recycle empty glass jars and bottles. Choose ones with a wide neck and wash them out well first in warm soapy water.

1 Brush glue all over the front of a cut out picture.

2 Slide a brush under the glued picture and lift it into an empty dry bottle. Press the picture against the glass and smooth down with the brush.

4 To make a stopper, roll a lump of air-hardening clay into a

3 Now add more pictures, leaving some space between them. When you have finished decorating the bottle, leave it overnight to give the glue time to dry.

ball between your hands. The rolled ball should be big enough to fit into the neck of the bottle.

76

5 Roll in glitter and glue on sequins to decorate. Leave overnight to dry.

6 Next day, fill the decorated bottle with salt and glue the stopper in place.

To decorate the bottles you can either buy Victorian picture scraps or cut pictures from magazines or printed wrapping papers.

Do make a stopper for the salt-filled bottles. You could use a table tennis or tennis ball instead of air-hardening clay.

You could tie a ribbon around the neck of the decorated jar or bottle to finish it off.

Boo!

Transform a cardboard crate into this terrific mask.

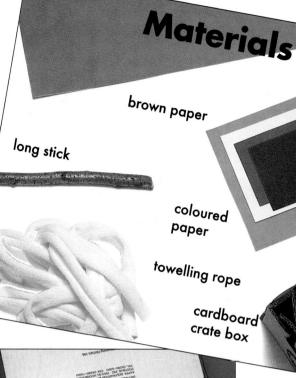

Materials

brown paper

long stick

coloured paper

towelling rope

cardboard crate box

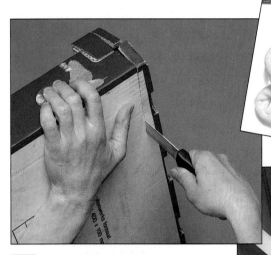

! **1** Ask an adult to cut the end off the box. A bread knife is probably best for this.

2 Mark a triangular point on to the cut end of the box.

! **3** Ask an adult to cut out the shape you have marked.

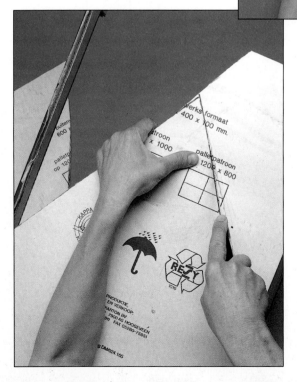

! **4** Ask an adult to score along the sides of the box at the base of the triangular shape.

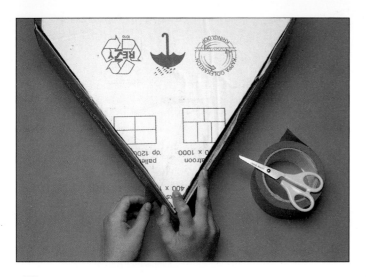

5 Bend the sides of the box in along the scored lines and tape them to the triangular shape with brown paper tape.

6 Cover the mask with brown paper. Cut shapes from coloured paper to make a face and glue in place.

Glue the towelling rope to the top of the mask to make hair. The finished mask, attached to a long stick, is big enough for two to hide behind.

Gift Boxes

Old boxes and containers decorated with cut-out paper shapes make lovely presents. So start collecting!

Materials

coloured paper

boxes

tissue-paper

1 Cover the box with plain paper. You can either use strips of paper or cut the paper exactly to fit.

2 Cut hearts and flower shapes from the tissue-paper.

3 Decorate the box with the cut out shapes glued in place.

4 To make the decorated box look shiny, brush all over with PVA glue. Leave to dry.

80

5 Cut leaves and flowers from the coloured paper. Stick the flowers on to the box. You can make the leaves stick up by putting glue on one end only.

6 Glue a circle of yellow tissue-paper to the centre of each flower.

You can decorate a box with shapes that have been cut and torn from tissue-paper and glued in place.

Fill the decorated boxes with sweets or biscuits and give as a gift.

Humpty Piñata

A delightful party game that can be played indoors or out.

Materials

white and black paper

2 small balloons

1 large balloon

string

magazines

ribbons

newspaper strips

sweets

! 1 Blow up the large balloon and tie a knot in the end. Brush the balloon with wallpaper paste and cover with newspaper strips. Add about 3 layers of newspaper strips pasting in between.

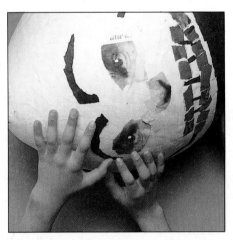

2 Tear the white and black paper into small strips. Paste the white squares over the top two-thirds of the balloon and the black squares over the bottom third so that the newspaper is completely hidden.

3 Glue pictures of a nose and eyes cut from magazines to Humpty's face. Make a mouth and eyebrows from torn coloured paper. Leave to dry for 24 hours. Deflate the balloon with a pin and remove.

4 Blow up the other 2 small balloons. Cut 2 strips from black paper and fold each into a concertina. Tape a balloon foot to each concertina leg and tape to Humpty. Tie a ribbon into a bow at each ankle.

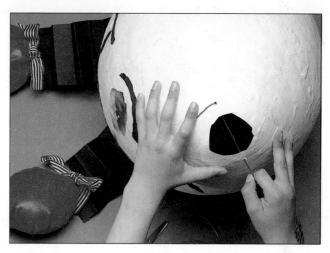

5 Cut an opening in the top of Humpty's head and push the sweets through it.

6 Pierce a hole on either side of the opening. Thread a length of string through the holes and tie a knot in each end.

Tie large colourful ribbons around Humpty's middle and hang him up from a tree outside or a doorway indoors.

Blindfold each child in turn and give him a wooden spoon to hold. Swing the Humpty piñata and then stand back. The blindfolded child now has 3 swipes at Humpty to try to break him open so that all his sweets scatter over the floor. When Humpty bursts everyone scrambles to see how many sweets they can pick up.

83

Pen Pals

Create your own matching stationery. Make sure the writing paper fits snugly into the envelope when it is folded in half or quarters.

1 Cut out some pictures from comics, magazines or printed wrapping papers.

2 Decorate the front of the envelope with the cut-out pictures and sticky stars. To re-use an old envelope, make sure that you cover the address and stamp.

With stationery that looks this good, everyone will want to get a letter from you.

3 Decorate the edges of the paper by sticking on cut-out pictures to match the envelope.

4 You can also glue on shapes torn from coloured paper, but do make sure that you leave enough space to write a message!

MAKING A SEAL
Pencil your initials *backwards* on to a small piece of card. Glue string along the pencil lines and leave to dry. To seal a used envelope mix flour and PVA glue into a paste and put a blob on to the flap. Press your initial stamp into the mixture and carefully lift off. Leave to dry before posting.

Mosaic

This picture is built up from squares of coloured paper.

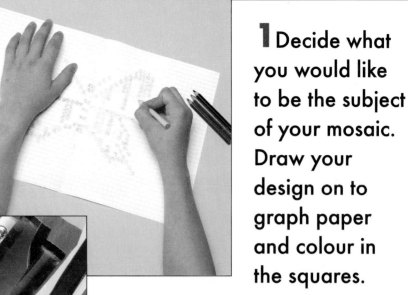

1 Decide what you would like to be the subject of your mosaic. Draw your design on to graph paper and colour in the squares.

2 Cut strips of paper the same width from all the different colours that you are going to need to complete your picture.

3 Cut the strips into small squares. Keep the colours separate.

4 Take a large sheet of paper and, following your graph paper design carefully, paste the coloured squares on to the paper to make your mosaic picture.

5 Try to keep the squares in even rows and columns. You may have to trim some of the squares as you go to keep them in line with each other.

TIP BOX
It's a good idea to draw a few lines on the paper up and down and across the page to help guide you as you make your mosaic.

When choosing a design for your mosaic, you will find that a symmetrical design is best.

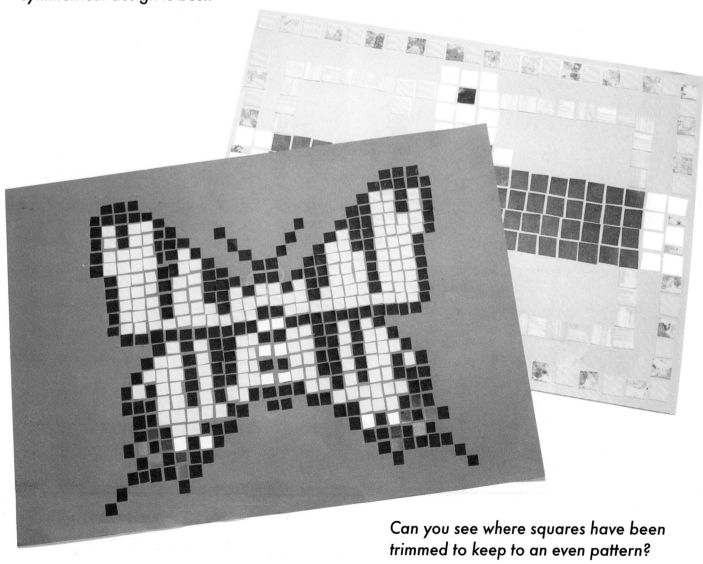

Can you see where squares have been trimmed to keep to an even pattern?

Dragon Kite

This tissue-paper kite will roar through the air on a breezy day.

Materials

coloured paper

2 garden sticks

string

tissue-paper

1 Make a cross from the 2 garden sticks and tie in the centre with string. Wind masking tape around the ends to make a raised edge.

2 Fold a long bit of string in half and loop around one point of the cross. Glue in place.

3 Loop the string around the second and third points of the cross, and pull tightly. Tie the ends of the string together at the fourth point. Secure the string at each point with a blob of glue and leave to dry.

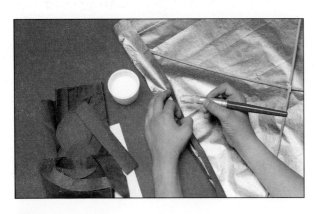

4 Glue tissue-paper over the front of the kite frame and decorate with eyes and a mouth cut from paper.

5 Cut slits along a piece of folded tissue-paper and tape under the mouth. Make another 2 and tape to the top corners.

6 To make the dragon's tail, tape together 2 pieces of tissue-paper. Fold in half lengthways and cut a wavy line along one edge. Open out and use tape to attach to the kite frame.

7 On the back of the kite frame tie 3 pieces of string each measuring about 30 cm to the middle and top 2 points of the frame. Knot the ends of the guide strings together.

You can add some decoration to the dragon's tail to make it look even more stunning.

Tie a small ball of string to the guide strings and you are ready to fly your kite.

Materials

large deep bowl

liquidizer

bucket

dried flowers

kitchen cloth

selection of papers

food colouring

net curtain

newspaper

2 wooden frames

drawing pins

glitter

tissue-paper

Paper Making

Paper making is fun to do, but it does take a little time to set up and you will need an adult's help.

⚠ **1** Cut a piece of net about 10 cm larger all around than the frame. Fold over each edge and pin to the sides of the frame making sure that the net is stretched tightly.

2 Tear or cut the paper into thin strips and pieces and put in to the bucket. Cover with water and soak overnight.

⚠ **3** Put a handful of soaked paper into the liquidizer adding more water when necessary. Liquidize for 15 seconds at a time until the pulp is creamy and well blended.

4 Put the blended pulp into a container that is larger than

the frame. Continue to liquidize the rest of the soaked paper until it has all been pulped. Add a little wallpaper paste to the pulped paper to help bind it together.

5 The pulped paper should not be as thick as porridge, but more like single or double cream. Add more water if necessary.

6 To make a couching bed to lay your homemade paper on to, place about 24 pages of newspaper on to a flat surface. Place a kitchen cloth on top of the newspaper.

7 Take the net-covered frame, **net side up**, and place the other frame on top of it.

8 Slowly lower the frames into the pulp and carefully lift back out again. You should not be able to see the net through the pulped paper. Drain the frames over the bowl.

Continues on next page

9 Take off the top frame and carefully place the net-covered frame, pulp side down, on to the couching bed. Press firmly with a cloth all over the net to wipe away any water.

If you want to make more than about 5 sheets of paper at a time you will need to make a second couching bed.

10 To loosen the paper from the net, gently rock the frame from side to side. If it sticks in places, give the back of the net more firm wipes.

11 Lift off the frame.

To make homemade paper you need paper, so start collecting all you can including old envelopes, newspapers, paper napkins, kitchen roll and computer paper.

12 You can add decorative materials to the paper such as tissue-paper shapes, dried flowers and glitter.

13 And you can use drops of food colouring to stain it different colours.

The paper will take about 24 hours to dry but you can speed this up by laying each sheet of paper, still sandwiched between its kitchen cloths, on to dry newspaper in a warm place. If the paper begins to curl as it dries, lay something heavy on top of it. Once the paper has dried, carefully peel away the kitchen cloth.

14 Before making a second sheet of paper, lay a kitchen cloth over the decorated paper, put several layers of newspaper on top, and finally another kitchen cloth. Continue from step 6.

Templates

For instructions on how to trace a template turn to page 96.

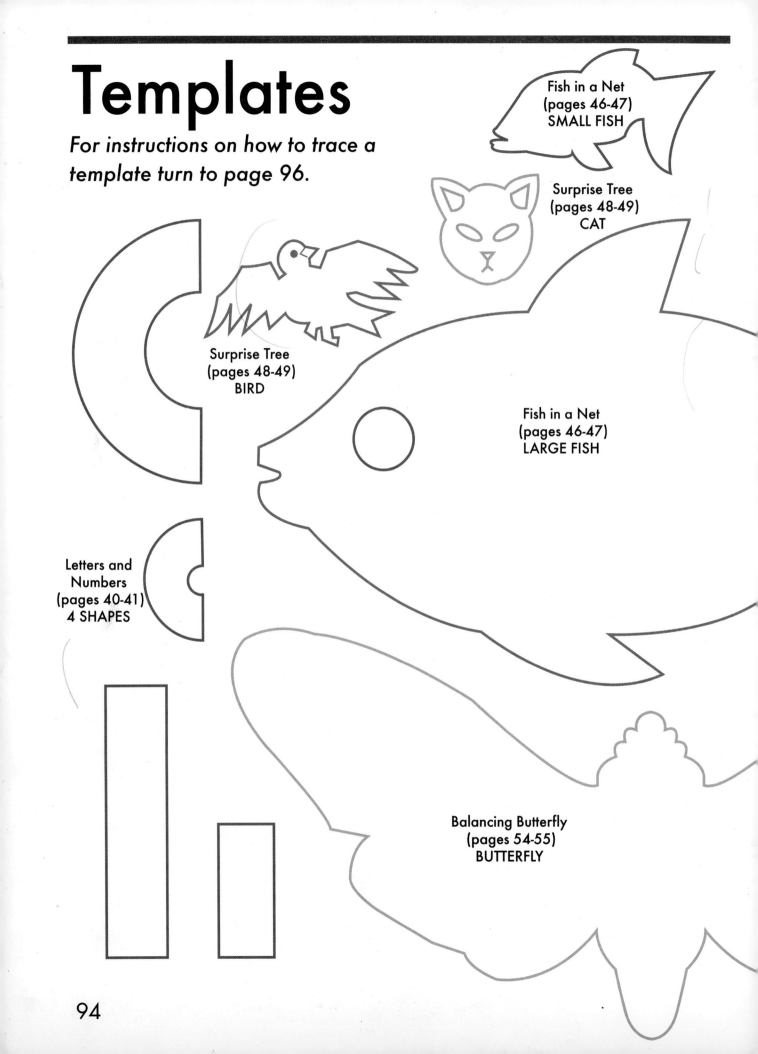

Fish in a Net
(pages 46-47)
SMALL FISH

Surprise Tree
(pages 48-49)
CAT

Surprise Tree
(pages 48-49)
BIRD

Fish in a Net
(pages 46-47)
LARGE FISH

Letters and
Numbers
(pages 40-41)
4 SHAPES

Balancing Butterfly
(pages 54-55)
BUTTERFLY

Circus Wagons
(pages 52-53)
LEOPARD

Circus Wagons
(pages 52-53)
LION

Dino Print
(pages 56-57)
FOOTPRINTS

Circus Wagons
(pages 52-53)
GIRAFFE

Dino Print
(pages 56-57)
DINOSAUR

95

Advice to Parents

Although children do painting at school, the time and materials they have there may be limited, and it may be difficult for them to work undisturbed. For children to explore the rich experience of painting they need room to stretch out, time to think and the opportunity to explore. When a child makes a painting, he or she dips a brush into paint and onto paper – a direct approach.

Print-making involves finding or making an object, which is then dipped into paint and onto the paper. There is an element of thinking and planning ahead in print-making, and this extra effort results in not just one painting, but the option for your child to produce a series of prints, or a combination of prints to create a completely different perspective.

The excitement of creating different perspectives and viewing familiar objects in a new way is also an important element of collage, where any material which is spare or disposable can be transformed into a work of art by your child. The information on this page is intended to help you and your child to get the most from painting, printing and collage projects.

Getting Ready

All that is required from you is an area of floor or table space where the child can work undisturbed, paint, a few basic tools and materials and your interest and encouragement. Spread newspapers over the table or work surface and the surrounding floor, especially if your child is working with an oil-based ink or paint. Your child should wear a plastic apron or a painting overall.

When rolling out printing ink, you must roll the ink out onto a completely flat surface. Use thick polythene sheeting or a flat piece of hardboard or an off-cut of plastic laminate or even a ceramic tile.

It is important to get ready for collage projects well in advance by starting to collect things that you would normally throw out, such as bits of paper, including newspapers, magazines, wrapping paper and wallpaper remnants, colourful labels and wrappers and cardboard. Encourage your child to add to this collection and provide him or her with a 'bits box' especially for this purpose.

Tools and Materials

Glue: Solvent-free adhesive is recommended, as it is versatile, clean, strong and safe. It is useful to have on hand a variety of glues suited to a range of different surfaces for collage projects. If using PVA as a varnish, try to make your collage on card, cardboard, wood or hardboard so that the paper doesn't curl too much. Glue stick won't wrinkle paper the way that water-based glues do. When you simply need to stick paper to paper, this type of glue is best.

Wallpaper paste: This is cheap and particularly useful for 3-dimensional projects such as making papier mâché. Follow the manufacturer's instructions and make up only a bit of the packet at a time to avoid waste.

Scissors: Children should use small scissors with round-ended, metal blades and plastic handles. Although these are fine for cutting paper and thin card, they will not cut thick card, and this is best done by you, using a craft knife. Use a metal ruler to provide a straight cutting edge. If you do not have a cutting mat, use an old chopping board or very thick card to protect the work surface beneath.

Varnish: When painting furniture, the surface is sealed with a light coat of varnish. Children should be supervised carefully when using varnish. Cover the work surface with newspaper, use in a well ventilated room, clean brushes with white spirit immediately after use and store the varnish carefully, as it is a flammable material.

Paint: Always have the basic set of colours in stock: red, blue, yellow, black and white. All other colours can be mixed from these.

Printing inks: Whenever the term printing ink is used in this book, you can use either water-soluble printing ink or paint.

Oil paints (used for marbling): You will need to clean children's hands and tools with a solvent such as methylated spirits, and make sure that they wash their hands thoroughly with warm, soapy water afterwards.

Roller: This is not an expensive tool and can be bought from any art and craft shop.

Paper: Paper can be expensive to buy, so do make a point of trying to re-use it wherever possible. Save cereal packets, clothes packaging, out-of-date calendars, etc.

Making a Tracing

To make a tracing from the templates on pages 94–95, lay a piece of tracing paper over the required template. Draw around the outline with a pencil. Turn over the paper and scribble over the pencil outline. Turn the tracing paper over once again and lay it down onto the paper or card to which you want to transfer the tracing. It is often a good idea to keep the tracing in place with masking tape. Carefully draw around the pencil outline, remove the tracing paper and go over the outline with black felt pen if necessary.

Clearing Up

Encourage your child to help you to clear up after painting, print-making or collage. Wash brushes, rollers and paint pots well. Store the dry brushes with the bristle ends upwards in a pot or jar. Methylated spirits should be used to wash out the brushes after the marbling project and this needs to be done by an adult.

The End Product

There is no 'right' way to do any of these projects. Art is about experimenting and seeing what happens. Do remember that all of the designs for the projects in this book are simply offered as guidelines. They are not meant to be copied exactly. Encourage children to develop their own ideas and to be proud of what they achieve.

First published 1995 by Merehurst Limited
Ferry House, 51–57 Lacy Road, Putney, London SW15 1PR

Copyright 1995 Merehurst Limited
ISBN 1 8980 18 45 6

Project Editor: Cheryl Brown
Designer: Anita Ruddell
Photography by: Jon Bouchier
Colour separation by P&W Graphics Pte Ltd, Singapore
Printed in Singapore by Toppan Printing Co.

The publisher would like to thank the staff and children of Riversdale Primary School, London Borough of Wandsworth for their help in producing the photographs for this book.